A Gift more precious than Gold

A CREATIVE GIFT BOOK

Creative Publishing
Abingdon Press

To
Andrew, Peter, Julia and Joanna

	Creative ISBN	*Abingdon ISBN*
A Gift more Precious than Gold	0 85081 060 5	0 687 27183 5

Published by Creative Publishing,
6 Pembroke Road, Moor Park,
Northwood, Middlesex, HA6 2HR, England

Published in the USA by Abingdon Press,
201 Eighth Avenue South, Nashville, Tennessee 37202

Printed in England by John Blackburn Ltd.

More precious than Gold

FOR MANY PEOPLE the enjoyment of God's Word seems at best a remote possibility. The Bible to them looks a big book, and feels an old book, especially those available in black covers. Even those editions with colour sections depicting Bible background present a problem; they look as if they belong to a different culture from the past and somewhere 'over there'.

To many church-going people, motivation to read the Holy Bible is also a problem. The temptation to listen to sermons and allow them to become the substitute for personal reading of God's Word is an all too frequent experience.

In producing this retelling of the 'gift more precious than gold' in God's Word we hope to have provided a 'bridge' that will enable many to discover the beauty, truth, hope and lasting encouragement which many have enjoyed from personal reading of God's Word.

A great deal of thought has gone into the visual presentation in order to give the maximum help, not only in reading and enjoying, but also in responding to God's Word.

A Gift More Precious than Gold can be used as a daily reading, either morning or evening. You can use it alongside your usual version of the Bible.

A Gift More Precious than Gold can also be read in sections. By looking at the contents pages you will see that the sections give progressive readings. By reading a complete section at a time important truths of the Bible will become clear.

A Gift More Precious than Gold is produced as a pocket book which has the benefit of being able to be slipped into a pocket or handbag quite easily.

Whether reading complete sections at a time, or being used as a daily reading aid, the following may be of help:

Read Expectantly. This is God's Word, so be prepared to receive new insights in his truth for you.

Read Deliberately. Time spent reflecting on what you've read will not be wasted. Meditation has always been a great strength in the development of Christian character.

Read Responsively. Besides the promises and blessings you can expect from the Holy Bible, there will also be challenges and new opportunities presented to you. By responding to God's Word your own life will be enriched.

Read Thankfully. God's Word is not meant to conceal God but reveal him. As you discover more about him and his wonderful promises to you, be thankful and enjoy everything he has in store for you.

It is the prayer of those who have been involved in bringing this book to you that you will discover the hope, encouragement, peace and love that only God, through his Son Jesus Christ, can bring you.

Robert F. Hicks

CONTENTS

BOOK A
Seeds of Love

BOOK B
Seeds of Joy

BOOK C
Seeds of Peace

BOOK D
Seeds of Hope

BOOK E
Seeds of Confidence

BOOK F
Seeds of Security

BOOK G
Seeds of Comfort

BOOK H
Seeds of Thanks

Seeds of Love

Remedy for life

The love of the Father

From the beginning of time God's loving
plans for us were that we should become his sons by
trusting in Jesus Christ. We are to be completely
whole and true, and are to live in love, thanking God
and praising him for freely giving us his loved
Son.   FROM EPHESIANS 1:4-6

1 Think how much love
God has richly poured on us—
he loves us so much
that he's made us his children!
Now we are his children—
and what we will be in the future
we don't yet know. But we do know
that when he comes again
we will be like him.
FROM 1 JOHN 3:1-3

2 Don't keep worrying about
how you will manage to find money
for food and clothes.
Look at the birds—
see how your Father in heaven
provides food for them.
Look at the flowers—
see the beautiful outfits
God has given them.
You are much more precious than birds.
God loves you
far more than he loves flowers.
FROM MATTHEW 6:25-34

 Even an evil earthly father gives good things to his
children, so your heavenly Father will most certainly
delight to give you good gifts.   FROM MATTHEW 7:11

The love of Jesus

Jesus Christ reveals truth faithfully. He was the first to rise from the dead and is the Ruler of all earthly rulers. He loves us and has set us free from all that we have done wrong by dying for us. He is the one who has all power and glory for ever.   FROM REVELATION 1:5

1 As Jesus walked along the road
two blind men kept calling out
above the shouts of the crowd:
'Jesus pity us, help us.'
Jesus stopped.
'What do you want?' he asked.
'To see,' they cried.
Lovingly Jesus touched their eyes
and at once they could see.
FROM MATTHEW 20:29-34

2 A leper came to Jesus for healing.
'If you want to, you can cure me,' he said.
Full of love and pity for the man,
Jesus said, 'I do want to.'
He touched the man
and immediately the leprosy was gone.
FROM MARK 1:40-42

3 When Jesus saw the crowds,
he was filled with love and sorrow for them
because they were lost, confused and muddled,
like sheep without a shepherd.
FROM MATTHEW 9:36

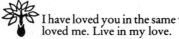 I have loved you in the same way that the Father has loved me. Live in my love.   FROM JOHN 15:9

A4

Searching Love

This is what the Lord says: 'I myself will
search for my sheep and keep them all within my
sight. I will rescue them and fetch them back from
wherever they are wandering in the mist and
dark.' FROM EZEKIEL 34:11

1 If you had a sheep that got lost
   you'd go and hunt for it, wouldn't you,
even though you had ninety-nine other sheep?
You would leave those ninety-nine sheep
and search for the lost sheep.
That's what it's like in heaven.
There is more delight over
   one lost and bad person
      who is sorry and comes back to God
   than over ninety-nine good people
      who do not need to turn back to God.
FROM LUKE 15:4,7

2 If a woman has ten valuable coins
   and has lost one of them,
does she not get a light
and sweep the house,
hunting until she finds it?
Then when it is found
she invites friends and neighbours
and says, 'Let's celebrate:
I've found my lost coin.'
Just the same, the angels
have a celebration
when one sinner turns back to God.
FROM LUKE 15:8-10

 God says, 'I will search out the lost sheep and bring
back the one that has strayed. The injured I will
bandage up and the weak I will strengthen.' FROM
EZEKIEL 34:16

Restoring love

Look how the Father lavishes his love on us. The extent of his love is so great that we are called God's children—that is who we really are. It stands to reason that those who don't know God do not recognise us either.   FROM 1 JOHN 3:1

1 'God said to his people,
I took you in my arms and taught you to walk.
I was the one who healed you with reins of love.
I led you into freedom.
I rescued you.
I fed you.'
FROM HOSEA 11:3-4

2 God said,
'I will heal their self-centredness.
I have stopped being angry with them
and I will love them freely.'
FROM HOSEA 14:4

3 God showed us how much he loves us
when he sent Jesus to us.
That is what true love is.
God loved us before we loved him.
FROM 1 JOHN 4:9-10

 He rescued us, but not because of any good thing that we had done, but because of his loving kindness. He renewed us by the Holy Spirit because we trust in Jesus so that we might look forward to true life.
FROM TITUS 3:5,7

The gift of love

God loved everyone so much that he gave his one and only Son, so that every person who turns to Jesus might not be destroyed but have true life for ever. He came to our world, not to be our judge, but to be our rescuer.   FROM JOHN 3:16-17

1 In Jesus' prayer to his Father
not long before he died
he spoke about his friends
and followers.
He said, 'I have told them about you,
and I will keep on
making you known to them
so that your love for me
may be in them,
and I myself may be in them.'
FROM JOHN 17:26

2 God has given his Holy Spirit to us
and with his Holy Spirit
he has poured out his love
into our hearts.
FROM ROMANS 5:5

3 Simon offered money so that he too
could give people the Holy Spirit.
Peter said to him:
'You and your money!
To think that you could buy
what God has given freely!'
FROM ACTS 8:18

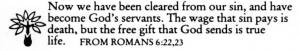
Now we have been cleared from our sin, and have become God's servants. The wage that sin pays is death, but the free gift that God sends is true life.   FROM ROMANS 6:22,23

God is love

FROM 1 JOHN 4:8

How we know love

Jesus said, 'If anybody really loves me he will do what I say. My Father will love him and we will come to him and stay with him. These words stem from my Father not from me.   FROM JOHN 14:23-24

1 Jesus said to his friends,
'Live in my love.
If you do what I say
you will live in my love,
just as I do what my Father says
and live in his love.'
This is what I want you to do:
love each other, as I have loved you.
FROM JOHN 15:9-10,12

2 Paul wrote to his friends,
'Seek to be completely good and whole.
Live together in harmony,
and God, who is full of love and peace,
will be with you.'
FROM 2 CORINTHIANS 13:11

3 Try out the loving kindness of God.
Taste and see how good he is.
The man who takes refuge in him
is happy.
FROM PSALM 34:8

 John wrote to his friends, 'When we love each other we know and experience God's complete love in us. By his Spirit we know that God lives in us and we live in him.'   FROM 1 JOHN 4:12-13

A14

The greatness of love

Your love, Lord, stretches up to the skies, your faithfulness reaches to the heavens; your goodness is as great as the mountains; your justice is deep as the oceans. You look after mankind and animals. How wonderful your never failing love is.   FROM PSALM 36:5-6

1 Paul wrote to the Ephesians:
'I pray that you may have
the strength and ability to grasp
how enormous Christ's love is—
how long and wide
and deep and tall it is.
I pray that you may experience
the love of Jesus, which is vaster
than all the knowledge in the world,
and cannot be plumbed
by man's mind.'
FROM EPHESIANS 3:18-19

2 John wrote,
'We are not afraid
to face God's judgement
because we live in his love.
Love is never afraid.
Perfect love drives fear away.'
FROM 1 JOHN 4:17-18

 Turn back to the Lord your God in your hearts; don't play act. For God is full of tenderness and love, slow to get angry and quick to relent.
FROM JOEL 2:13

Love for one another

We are able to love, because God loved us in the first place. If you say that you love God while you are full of hate for someone you know, you are talking rubbish. God has given us a clear command: if you love God, you must love your fellow Christians. FROM 1 JOHN 4:20-21

1 Jesus said,
'I am giving you new instructions:
love each other.
Love each other in the way I have loved you.
Everyone will know that you belong to me
if you love each other.'
FROM JOHN 13:34-35

2 Christian friends,
what's the point in claiming to have faith,
if you have nothing to show for it?
If a brother or sister is starving or naked
and you tell him,
'Have a good day, don't go hungry or get
cold,'
but you don't lift a finger to help,
what good are you doing?
So faith without deeds is a dead loss.
FROM JAMES 2:14-17

 John, known as the apostle of love, wrote, 'Dear friends, since God has loved us so much, we really must love each other. God lives in us when we love each other.' FROM 1 JOHN 4:11-12

Love in action

You deceive yourselves if you think all you have to do is just listen to God's message; you have to do what it tells you. If you hear the word and then ignore it, you're like a person who looks at himself in a mirror and then forgets what he looks like.

FROM JAMES 1:22-24

1 When Jesus and his friends met
for their last meal together,
this is what Jesus suddenly did.
He stood up, took off his outer clothing
and tied a towel round his waist.
He poured water into a bowl and started
washing and drying his friends' dirty feet.
When he had finished he said,
'I did this to show you how you should live.
You must not be high and mighty
but must humbly care for one another,
and look after each other,
doing menial tasks for each other.'

FROM JOHN 13:4-15

2 Love doesn't get fed up and irritable.
Love doesn't hanker after
other people's possessions or lifestyle.
Love isn't big-headed, or bad-mannered.
Love doesn't sulk and harbour grudges.

FROM 1 CORINTHIANS 13:4-5

Through love, give yourselves over to helping one another, for all God's law is summed up in the one command to love your neighbour as yourself. So stop all that destructive nastiness and backbiting.

FROM GALATIANS 5:13-15

Love for ever

God said, 'I will never stop loving you, no matter what happens. In the middle of an earthquake that makes mountains and hills crash to the ground my love will be steady. Not a tremor will disturb my binding love and peace.'   FROM ISAIAH 54:10

1 The Lord said, 'I have loved you with a love that never gives up.
I have led you with love and kindness.'
FROM JEREMIAH 31:3

2 Paul wrote,
'Nothing will ever be able to cut me off from God's love.
I know this for certain.
There is no power in heaven or on earth,
no evil force, no demon, no angel,
nothing in the future or the past
nothing in the remotest constellation
or deepest cavern.
Nothing can separate me from God's love—
not even death itself can do this.'
FROM ROMANS 8:35-39

3 Give thanks to the Lord God for he is good.
His love knows no end.
FROM PSALM 136:1-2

 Give thanks to the Lord of the universe, for the Lord is good. His love never comes to an end, but goes on for ever and ever.   FROM JEREMIAH 33:11

Prayers of love

We thank you Lord Jesus that though you were
rejected, despised, persecuted and crucified, you
never stopped loving anybody. How we thank you
for your eternal and unfailing love. We pray that
through your Holy Spirit you will help us to love
each other as you love us.
Amen.

Thank you for your immense love for me, Lord. It is
so enormous that I cannot really grasp just how much
you love me. Thank you, Lord, that your love will
endure for ever, and that nothing can separate me
from it.
Amen.

My own prayer

_____

_____

_____

Seeds of
Joy

Quality in living

The promise of joy

Jesus said, 'Father, I will soon be returning to you, but I am speaking to them now, while I am still in this world, so that their hearts may be full of my joy. Make them holy through your word. Your word is truth.'   FROM JOHN 17:13,17

1 Jesus said:
'Everyone around you will be happy
and you will be sad.
But your sadness will turn into joy.
I shall see you again,
and your hearts will be full of joy.
And no one will be able to take away your joy.'
FROM JOHN 16:20,22

2 Jesus said:
'As the Father has loved me,
so I have loved you.
    Remain in my love.
If you obey my commands,
    you will remain in my love,
just as I have obeyed
my Father's commands
    and remain in his love.
I am telling you this so that my own joy may be in you, and your joy be complete.
FROM JOHN 15:9-11

 Let us praise Jesus Christ because he has the power to keep you from falling, and to bring you to God without fault and with great joy.   FROM JUDE 24

Joy is from God

What the Spirit brings is very different from what the world brings. From the Spirit come love, joy, peace; patience, kindness, goodness; faithfulness, gentleness and self-control. Since the Spirit gives life to us, we must let him direct our lives. FROM GALATIANS 5:22-23, 25

1 I pray that the God of hope will fill you with great joy and peace, and hope, by the Holy Spirit's power.
FROM ROMANS 15:13

2 You will show me the path that leads to life. Your presence will fill me with joy and bring me pleasure for ever.
PSALM 16:11

3 Although God's word was spreading like wildfire, Paul and Barnabas were hounded out of town. But the new Christians left behind in Antioch were filled with joy and the Holy Spirit.
FROM ACTS 13:49-52

 I want you to be always full of joy in the Lord. I will say it again: be joyful! My God will give you everything you need from the treasure-house of riches that are yours in Jesus Christ.
FROM PHILIPPIANS 4:4, 19

Inner joy

God made a promise to Abraham his servant, and he never broke it. As he led his people out from slavery in Egypt they sang aloud with joy. God's own people rejoiced.   FROM PSALM 105:42-43

1 You have within you strength from God's glorious power, so that you have patience and endurance. You are able to bear everything joyfully, thanking the Father who made you fit to share his kingdom of light.
FROM COLOSSIANS 1:11-12

2 I am always aware of God's presence near me, and nothing can shake me. That is why I am thankful and glad, and feel completely secure.
FROM PSALM 16:8-9

3 Come let us praise God!
Let us sing aloud
for joy
to God
who protects us.
FROM PSALM 95:1-2

 With all my heart, I praise you Lord God. I will sing with joy, because of you. I will sing praise to you, almighty God.   FROM PSALM 9:1-2

Joy always

Be always joyful; never stop praying. Give thanks to God for all things, no matter what happens to you, because this is how God wants you to live with Jesus Christ. Never damp down the Holy Spirit.   FROM 1 THESSALONIANS 5:16-18

1 God did not leave you without evidence of himself. You can see him at work in the good things he does for you. He has shown his kindness by sending rain and giving crops in each season. He gives you food, and fills your heart with happiness.
FROM ACTS 14:17

2 I will be glad because of the Lord.
I will be happy because he saved me.
With all my heart
I will say to God,
'There is no one like you.
    You rescue
        the weak
            and poor
    from their oppressors.'
FROM PSALM 35:9-10

 We offer ourselves to you as God's servants. We have good reason to be sad yet we rejoice all the time. We are poor, yet we make many spiritually rich.   FROM 2 CORINTHIANS 6:4,10

Joy in faith

Everybody who comes to you for shelter will be kept safe. Your people will always be singing with joy. You cover them with your power so they rejoice. You shield the righteous and surround them with your happiness.   FROM PSALM 5:11-12

1 Jesus said,
'I am telling you the truth.
Whatever you ask the Father
in my name
he will give you.
So far
you have asked nothing in my name.
  Ask
    and you will receive,
      so your joy will be complete.'
FROM JOHN 16:23-24

2 You did not see him
  yet you love him.
And you still believe him
without seeing him.
So you are already filled
with joy so marvellous
that it cannot be described,
since you are receiving
the salvation of your souls.
This is the reason
for your faith in him.
FROM 1 PETER 1:8-9

 Don't be lazy, but keep on serving the Lord. Your hope in Jesus will keep you joyful, so be patient through troubles and keep on praying.   FROM ROMANS 12:12

My soul is full of joy
FROM LUKE 1:47

Joy in God's saving plan

We have peace with God because of our trust in our Lord Jesus Christ. Because of Jesus, we now know about God's loving kindness at first hand. We also know that we shall have a share in God's glory, and so we rejoice.   FROM ROMANS 5:1-2

1 There is more joy in heaven
over one sinner who turns from his evil ways
than over ninety-nine respectable people
who do not feel they need to turn to God.
FROM LUKE 15:7

2 I tell you, the angels of God
rejoice over the one sinner
who turns from his wrongdoing to God.
FROM LUKE 15:10

3 Give me back the joy
that comes from following you.
Make me happy to obey your will.
Then I'll teach your commands to others so
that they too can turn to you, asking you to
forgive them.
FROM PSALM 51:12-13

 We are filled with joyful trust in God through the Lord Jesus. It is Jesus who has brought us into friendship with God.   FROM ROMANS 5:10-11

Sing for joy

Let all who find safety in you rejoice. May they always sing for joy. They are really happy because you protect them, O Lord. You bless those who are seeking to obey you. You protect and defend them with your love.   FROM PSALM 5:11

1 Praise God with shouts of joy.
Sing praises to him. Say to him:
'Everything you do is wonderful.'
FROM PSALM 66:1-3

2 I will go to your altar, Lord God,
for you are the source of my joy.
There I will play my harp
and sing praises to you, my God.
FROM PSALM 43:4

3 God's love is constant and surrounds all
those who place their trust in him. You
who are right before God, be glad! Rejoice,
because of what God has done for you. If you
obey him, then shout aloud for joy!
FROM PSALM 32:10-11

 May all those who obey God sing with joy in their hearts as they enjoy his presence. May they sing joyfully because they are happy.   FROM PSALM 68:3

Joy from Jesus

Jesus could not be held down by death. He broke away from its grip when God raised him up. King David spoke about Jesus' coming victory. He said, 'I saw the Lord before me and rejoiced with my heart and voice. I'll find complete joy in his company.' FROM ACTS 2:24-26,28

1 The shepherds were afraid, but the angel said,
'Do not be afraid.
I bring good news.
Great joy is coming to all the people.
For today, in David's city,
a Saviour has been born to you—
Christ Jesus the Lord.'
FROM LUKE 2:9-11

2 The women who saw the angel
at Jesus' empty tomb
were filled with joy,
and ran to tell the others.
FROM MATTHEW 28:8

3 We give thanks to the God and Father
of our Lord Jesus Christ.
In his great mercy
he has given us new life and hope
because we trust in Jesus
whom God raised from the dead.
FROM 1 PETER 1:3,6

Mary said, 'My heart overflows with praise to the Lord. Because of God my Saviour my soul is full of joy. He has not forgotten me, his humble servant. FROM LUKE 1:46-47

Joy through Suffering

If you share in Christ's suffering, you can be glad because when his glory is revealed you will overflow with joy. If you are mocked for being a Christian you can be happy for it is then that God's Spirit is with you.　　FROM 1 PETER 4:13-14

1 In our sorrows we have always cause for joy.
FROM 2 CORINTHIANS 6:10

2 Let us get rid of everything that hinders us from following Jesus, and most of all, let us throw out the sins which keep tripping us up.
Let us keep our eyes trained on Jesus who sees us through all the way.
He was able to withstand a terrible death on the cross, because he kept the thought of his future joy in his mind.
FROM HEBREWS 12:1-2

3 You accepted joyfully the confiscation of your possessions because you knew that you owned something that was better and more lasting.
FROM HEBREWS 10:34

The Lamb who sits on the throne will be their shepherd and will lead them to springs of fresh water; and God will wipe all tears from their eyes.
FROM REVELATION 7:17

Joy is for Sharing

Offering thanks to the Lord is the order of the day. Praise the Lord for all the wonderful things he has done, and for his continuous love. Thank him by giving yourself to him and tell others, with songs of joy. FROM PSALM 107:21-22

1 Each day they met together in the temple. In their homes, they broke bread and ate together, sharing their meals with joyful open hearts.
FROM ACTS 2:46

2 The nations of the world should be glad. They should sing for joy because, Lord, you rule them with justice and you guide them.
FROM PSALM 67:4

3 They worshipped Jesus as he ascended to heaven. Then they returned to Jerusalem, filled with deep joy. They spent all their time in the temple, giving thanks to God.
FROM LUKE 24:52-53

The Lord takes pleasure in his people. He brings victory to those who depend on him. Let God's people rejoice together and sing joyfully all night long. FROM PSALM 149:4-5

Prayers for joy

Dear God, I know that when I trust and believe in you, I do not dwell on grief or pain, but abide in a deep joy in your presence. Thank you that this is what you promised in your word, and that I can come to you and know real, lasting joy.
Amen.

How you are to be glorified, Lord! How we praise you for the joy in our hearts because of you, Lord. We do thank you that we are able to praise and worship you freely, with all our hearts, in the fullness of the joy you give to us.
Amen.

My own prayer

_____

_____

_____

$\mathcal{S}$eeds of
Peace

Healing for all

Promise of peace with God

Listen, the Lord Almighty is speaking, 'Glory will fill this house of God. The glory of this new house of God will be greater than the glory of the old house,' says the almighty God. 'In this new era of my rule, I will grant peace,' declares God.

FROM HAGGAI 2:9

1 To us a child is born,
to us a son is given,
and upon his shoulders
will rest all authority.
He will be called
wonderful counsellor,
mighty God,
everlasting Father,
prince of peace.

FROM ISAIAH 9:6

2 Suddenly a great throng
of the heavenly host was with the angel.
They were praising God and saying:
'Glory to God
in the highest heaven
and peace to men
on whom his favour rests.'

FROM LUKE 2:13-14

 The God of peace will soon crush Satan under your feet. May the free and undeserved love of our Lord Jesus be with you.   FROM ROMANS 16:20

Peace from God the Father

In the tender mercy of our God heaven's dawn will rise upon us to give light to those who live in darkness and under death's shadow, and to guide our feet in the way of peace.   FROM LUKE 1:78-79

1 May the God of peace,
who brought our Lord Jesus,
the great Shepherd of the sheep,
back from the dead,
give you every good gift that you need
to do his will.
FROM HEBREWS 13:20-21

2 Grace and peace in fullest measure
will be yours as you grow deeper
in the knowledge of God
and our Lord Jesus.
FROM 2 PETER 1:2

3 To everyone in Rome
who is loved by God
and is called to be a saint—
may grace be yours,
may peace be yours,
from our Father God
and from the Lord Jesus Christ.
FROM ROMANS 1:7

Make perfection your aim; have the same goals; be at peace among yourselves. Then God's love and God's peace will be with you.   FROM 2 CORINTHIANS 13:11

Living in peace

From Jude, James' brother and servant of
Jesus Christ. To those who have been called by God
and are loved by him and who are kept safe by Jesus
Christ. May you be filled to overflowing with God's
loving kindness and his peace and love.
FROM JUDE 1-2

1 Surely God's salvation is near
to those who are his;
love and faithfulness meet together,
goodness and peace embrace.
FROM PSALM 85:9-10

2 The wisdom that comes from God
is first of all pure.
It is then peace-loving
    and kindly,
considerate
    and open to reason,
full of compassion and good deeds.
It is straightforward and sincere.
Peacemakers sow seeds
which bear the fruit of goodness.
FROM JAMES 3:17-18

3 So, to all of you who are loved by God,
grace and peace are yours
from God the Father and the Lord Jesus.
FROM ROMANS 1:7

 We pray that you may have the grace and peace
which come from God our Father, and the Lord
Jesus Christ. Because of Christ we are freed from our
sin.   FROM GALATIANS 1:3

Peace to others

If somebody has wronged you, you should not try to get your own back. Your behaviour must be completely above board. You must do all within your power to live at peace with everyone.
FROM ROMANS 12:17-18

1 Happy are the peacemakers:
God shall call them his sons.
Happy are those who have suffered
for the cause of right:
the kingdom of Heaven is theirs.
FROM MATTHEW 5:9,10

2 Instead of giving in to wrong desires,
run away from them.
Pursue things that are
    good
       and right
          and just,
what is of faith,
    love,
       and peace.
Search for these,
in company with all those who sincerely seek
God's help.
FROM 2 TIMOTHY 2:22

 So in every way we can let us work for peace. Let us concentrate on supporting and encouraging each other. Don't argue over out-of-date food laws and ruin what God has done.　　FROM ROMANS 14:19

Seek Peace

Live a life of peace with each other. Warn those who are work shy, draw alongside the timid, be a tower of strength to the weak, and show patience to everyone.   FROM 1 THESSALONIANS 5:13

1 A gentle answer turns away anger, but a harsh reply stirs it up.
FROM PROVERBS 15:1

2 Remember,
anyone who wants to enjoy life
and see good days
must control his tongue,
and not deal in double talk.
In no circumstances
must he allow evil to succeed,
but only good.
He must seek wholeness and harmony,
and pursue it.
FROM 1 PETER 3:10-11

3 Do everything you can
to live at peace with everyone,
and to live a holy life,
because we will never see the Lord
without holiness.
FROM HEBREWS 12:14

 Don't let evil words pass your lips. Cut out all lying. Turn from evil and do good; seek peace and pursue it.   FROM PSALM 34:13-14

God's peace will be with you
FROM 2 CORINTHIANS 13:11

Peace is from Jesus

It is by Jesus Christ, who is Lord of all, that the good news of peace came. God sent this message to his people. The message started with John the Baptist in Galilee and then spread all over Judea.
FROM ACTS 10:36-37

1 Jesus appeared and stood among the disciples.
He said, 'Peace be with you.'
Seven days later,
when the disciples were again in the house
with all the doors locked
Jesus came once more.
He stood in the middle of them and said,
'Peace be with you.'
FROM JOHN 20:19, 26

2 'I have told you this so that
you may find your peace in me.
You will have this peace
when you keep close to me.
In the world you will have many troubles,
but take courage,
I have won the victory
over the world.'
FROM JOHN 16:33

 'Peace I leave with you; my own peace I give you. I do not give it to you as the world does. Don't be worried, or upset, or afraid.'   FROM JOHN 14:27

Peace from God's Spirit

People who live their lives in line with God's Spirit have their minds trained on the Spirit's wishes. It is death to focus on what is unspiritual. Life and peace can only come when the mind is controlled by the Spirit.   FROM ROMANS 8:5,6

1 But what fruit the Spirit produces!
Love,
joy,
   peace,
      patience,
         kindness
            faithfulness,
               gentleness,
                  and self control.
FROM GALATIANS 5:22-23

2 Bear with one another.
Be gentle, humble and patient.
Show your love
by helping each other.
Let the Spirit bind you together
in loving harmony.
FROM EPHESIANS 4:2-3

 For those who belong to God, old laws about food and drink are not important. Rather belonging to God means goodness, peace and joy in the power of the Holy Spirit.   FROM ROMANS 14:17

Peace with God

So, we see that since we have been put right with God through faith in our Lord Jesus Christ, we have peace with God. As we put our trust in Jesus we know God's undeserved and free love for us.   FROM ROMANS 5:1-2

1 Through Jesus, the whole universe
is restored to God.
God made peace
when his Son died on the cross,
and everything in heaven and on earth was
brought back to himself.
FROM COLOSSIANS 1:20

2 Now, in Christ Jesus,
you who were once far away from God
have been brought near to him
because of the death of Jesus.
For it is Jesus who has restored peace
between us and God,
and between us and our fellow men.
He has united us
by breaking down
the barrier created by sin and enmity
that separated us.
FROM EPHESIANS 2:13-15

 Paul wrote to his friends at Philippi, 'Follow my example in what I have said and done. Then God's peace will be yours.'   FROM PHILIPPIANS 4:9

Peace Within

Let people see that you have a gentle spirit. Remember that the Lord is coming soon. The peace of God which is beyond our understanding will guard your hearts and minds through the power of Jesus Christ.   FROM PHILIPPIANS 4:5,7

1 And let the peace of Christ hold sway
in your hearts and minds,
because you are all part of the body of Christ,
and he wants you to live in peace.
FROM COLOSSIANS 3:15

2 May God, the source of hope,
fill you with such joy and peace
as you trust him, that by the power of the
Holy Spirit
hope may flow out from you.
FROM ROMANS 15:13

3 A woman in need of healing
touched the edge of Jesus' cloak
and was made well.
Then she came and knelt down
in front of Jesus,
and Jesus said to her,
'Your faith has made you well.
Go in peace.'
FROM LUKE 8:43-48

 You are being made holy by the death of Jesus Christ in order that you may obey him. May you be richly filled with his grace and peace.   FROM 1 PETER 1:2

The Gift of Peace

My prayer for you Thessalonian Christians is this: I pray that the peace which springs from the Lord himself may be yours; may his peace be your experience wherever you are, and in whatever you do. May the Lord of peace stay with you all.   FROM 2 THESSALONIANS 3:16

1 From John,
to the seven churches of Asia:
grace and peace be yours from God,
  who is,
  who was,
  and who is to come,
and from the seven spirits
in front of his throne,
and from Jesus Christ.
Jesus is totally trustworthy;
he is the first person
to be raised from the dead;
and now he rules in heaven
over all the world's rulers.
FROM REVELATION 1:4-5

 Paul wrote these words at the end of a letter: 'May God himself, the God of peace, make you clean and whole through and through, and keep you till Jesus comes again. God is completely reliable. He called you to himself, and he will do it.
FROM 1 THESSALONIANS 5:23,24

Prayers for peace

Lord God, I confess to you that I am often quick to anger, impatient, sharp-tongued and harsh. I pray, Lord, that you will instil in me a sense of peace, that I may live in harmony with others, as you showed us by your example.
Amen.

'Life and peace can only come when the mind is controlled by the Spirit.'
Lord, in the middle of the rush and bustle of the world, we crave a time when we can be with you quietly. Let your Spirit enter us, Lord, so that we can be at rest and at peace with you.
Amen.

My own prayer

_____

_____

_____

Seeds of
Hope

Certainty for tomorrow

Promise of Hope

The Lord Almighty gives you this wonderful promise: 'You will be my very own sons and daughters. I will be like a caring father to you.' It is because we have these promises of hope that we can say no to all that is not from God, and make it our aim to please God in all we do.   FROM 2 CORINTHIANS 6:18-7:1

1 Faith is being sure that we will receive what we hope for.
It is being certain of things we cannot see.
It is because they had faith that the men of old were approved by God.
FROM HEBREWS 11:1,2

2 When there seemed no hope, Abraham still believed and hoped.
He became the father of many nations, exactly as it had been promised him:
'Your descendants shall be many.'
FROM ROMANS 4:18-21

3 Having the glorious hope of new life through God's Spirit
we can be very bold indeed.
By God's Spirit we can freely draw near to God.
We reflect God's splendour like mirrors by God's Spirit in us.
FROM 2 CORINTHIANS 3:13,18

 The Psalmist shows his faith in God with this request: 'Remember your word of promise to me. It has given me hope. Your promise refreshes my soul.   FROM PSALM 119:49-50

Hope from God

The scriptures again and again encourage us to rejoice and praise God. Paul wrote, 'May the God of hope fill you with all joy and peace in believing, so that by the power of the Holy Spirit you may overflow with hope.   FROM ROMANS 15:13

1 Through Jesus you now have faith in God,
who raised him from the dead
and glorified him,
so that your faith and hope
are in God alone.
FROM 1 PETER 1:21

2 The Lord God promised:
'Those who hope in me shall not be let down.'
FROM ISAIAH 49:23

3 Here then are two unalterable facts:
God's promise
and God's oath.
It is impossible for God to lie.
So we can take new courage,
being sure without doubt
of the hope God offers us.
FROM HEBREWS 6:18-19

 I do not trust in anyone other than God himself. My hope only comes from him. He is my rock and fortress and salvation.   FROM PSALM 62:5-6

Hope to the very end

We give thanks to God, the Father of our Lord Jesus Christ. It is because of his great mercy that we have hope. And this hope lives in us because of Jesus' resurrection. So we look forward to heaven, where all of God's blessings are kept safe for us.   FROM 1 PETER 1:3-4

1 Our one desire is for everyone
to show the same eager concern
to the very end
when your hope will become reality.
Do not grow tired, but copy those who,
with faith and persistent patience,
possess the promises.
FROM HEBREWS 6:11-12

2 Suffering brings patience,
which in turn produces perseverance.
And this we know results in hope,
which does not disappoint us.
For God's love is poured into our hearts
by his Holy Spirit in us.
FROM ROMANS 5:3-5

 In faith, by the help of God's Spirit, we eagerly wait to receive the righteousness for which we hope. Faith with love is the key to following Jesus.
FROM GALATIANS 5:5-6

Hope through despair

Paul said about his illness, 'Three times I asked God to remove it. But God said, 'You will know my perfect power in the midst of your weakness.' So I want to tell everyone about my weaknesses, because it is then that I know about Christ's care for me. When I am weak, I am really strong.'   FROM 2 CORINTHIANS 12:9-10

1 As the deer pants
for streams of water,
so my soul pants for you, my God.
I thirst within for the living God.
FROM PSALM 42:1-2

2 My soul is downcast within me,
so I will turn to God.
Deep calls to deep,
in the roar of your waterfalls.
Your waves break and sweep over me.
By day, the Lord directs his love,
at night his song stays with me.
He is the God of my life.
FROM PSALM 42:6-8

 My soul, why are you so downcast? Why am I so disturbed within? Put your hope in God. I will still praise him, for he is my Saviour.   FROM PSALM 43:5

Looking to a different life

How wonderful is the love the Father has given to us so freely. The extent of this love is seen in that we are called God's children. When God comes again, and we see him, we will be like him. It is because we have this hope that we try to be pure, just like God.   FROM 1 JOHN 3:1-3

1 Free your mind,
be ready to act.
Set your hope completely
on the grace which will be yours
when Christ Jesus is revealed.
FROM 1 PETER 1:13

2 It is only when we obey
God's commands
that we can be sure
that we know him.
FROM 1 JOHN 2:3

3 For in this life
there is no city that endures;
we seek a city
that is still to come.
Keep doing good deeds
and share what you have.
These are the kind of sacrifices
God is pleased with.
FROM HEBREWS 13:14,16

There is only one Spirit, and there is only one body of believers. In a similar way you have but one hope, the hope of belonging to God.
FROM EPHESIANS 4:4

May the God of hope fill you
FROM ROMANS 15:13

Hope in Jesus

Matthew said that Jesus fulfilled this prophecy from Isaiah: 'He is one I have specially selected, my servant whom I chose. I love him, and I take delight in him and he has my Spirit. People from all over the world will place their hope in him.' FROM MATTHEW 12:18-21

1 Paul began his letter to Timothy with the words:
'Paul, an apostle of Christ Jesus,
appointed by command of God our Saviour
and Christ Jesus our hope,
to Timothy, my son in our faith.'
FROM 1 TIMOTHY 1:1

2 It was God's purpose to make known to the Gentiles
the glorious riches of his secret plans which are:
Christ in you,
the hope of all that is yet to come!
FROM COLOSSIANS 1:27

3 We are the house God is building
and Jesus is the Son and Lord of the house.
But we must hold on to our courage
and hope in Jesus.
FROM HEBREWS 3:6

 We have been specially selected to live with Jesus. It was planned this way before the dawn of time, that we should hope in Christ, and live to praise him. FROM EPHESIANS 1:11-12

God's word gives hope

I am so happy to follow your ways. I think carefully about your commands and ponder your directions. Lord, you are my shield and the place where I am kept safe. I have placed my hope and trust in your word.   FROM PSALM 119:14-15, 114

1 Simply acknowledge Christ in your hearts.
Always have your answer ready
for people who ask you the reason
for the hope that you have.
FROM 1 PETER 3:15

2 Let us put on faith and love
as a coat of mail,
and the hope of salvation
for a helmet.
FROM 1 THESSALONIANS 5:8

3 If you have hope,
keep joyful.
Be patient
in times of trouble
and pray always.
FROM ROMANS 12:12

Everything written in the Scriptures long ago was written to teach us patience and endurance and to encourage us so that we might have hope.
FROM ROMANS 15:4

Hope is not blind

Our faith has a solid foundation for it rests in the hope of eternal life, which was promised from the dawn of time by God. True to his promise God has revealed this hope and commanded me to preach it.   FROM TITUS 1:2-3

1 May God,
the Father of our Lord Jesus Christ,
give you his Spirit of wisdom
and revelation:
to bring you to full knowledge of him.
May God open the eyes of your mind
so that you may know the hope
to which he has called you;
and the rich splendour
he has promised
to those who are his.
FROM EPHESIANS 1:17-18

2 The love you show to all fellow believers
springs from the hope which is stored up
for you in heaven.
FROM COLOSSIANS 1:5

3 Tell rich people
not to place their hope on their wealth,
which cannot be relied on,
but on God
who gives to us generously and richly.
FROM 1 TIMOTHY 6:17

 When we give God the honour he deserves we make him glad. God is pleased when we place our hope in his faithful love.   FROM PSALM 147:11

Future hope

We should be pitied more than anybody else if we have hope in Christ for only this life. But the truth of the matter is that at the end of this world order, God will take over and everything will be in his hands. We know this because Jesus rose from the dead.   FROM 1 CORINTHIANS 15:19-25

1 Our eyes will see the new Jerusalem,
   a peaceful permanent home,
it will be like a rich pasture land
with broad rivers and streams.
Our Lord God will be there,
our Mighty One.
The Lord is our King
who will save us.
In the new Jerusalem
no one will say, 'I am ill,'
and all who live there
will be forgiven their sins.
FROM ISAIAH 33:20-24

2 Then I saw a new heaven and a new earth
   for the first had passed away.
I saw the holy city,
the new Jerusalem,
coming from God.
I heard a loud voice from the throne saying,
'Now the home of God is with men.
He will live with them,
and be their God.'
FROM REVELATION 21:1-3

 When the Lord Jesus returns, Christians who have already died will rise first; and then we who are still alive will be caught up together, to be with the Lord.   FROM 1 THESSALONIANS 4:16-17

Hope realised

These words are from the faithful and true witness, from the one responsible for all of God's creation: 'To him who overcomes, who is not defeated, I will give the right to sit with me on my throne, just as I overcame and sat down with my Father on his throne.'   FROM REVELATION 3:14,21

1 In my vision at night
I saw before me one like a son of man
coming down with the clouds.
His rule is everlasting.
It will not pass away.
His kingdom will never be destroyed.
He was given authority, glory,
kingly power.
All peoples and nations worshipped him.
FROM DANIEL 7:13-14

2 Jesus said:
'Not everyone who repeats to me the words,
'Lord, Lord',
will enter the kingdom of heaven,
but only the person
who obey the commands
of my Father in heaven.'
FROM MATTHEW 7:21

 We eagerly wait a Saviour from heaven, the Lord Jesus Christ. He will change our bodies so that they will be like his glorious body.
FROM PHILIPPIANS 3:20-21

Prayers of hope

In the world today, Lord, amidst trouble and despair, we need someone on whom we can rely. Thank you, Lord, for the hope you offer our sad world; a real, living hope that we can turn to and be satisfied by. Amen.

I thank you, Lord, for your word which you have given for me. Thank you for all it teaches me, and for the hope which your scripture brings. I pray that you will continue to speak to me through the scriptures, so that I may gain even greater encouragement from them.
Amen.

My own prayer

_____

_____

_____

Seeds of Confidence

Strength for today

The seeds of trust

Lord, may light from your face shine on us.
My heart is full of greater joy than food and drink can
ever give. I lie down and fall asleep peacefully, for
you, Lord, and you alone, make me know that I am
safe.   FROM PSALM 4:6-8

1 Trust in the Lord and do good;
then you will live safely.
Seek your happiness in the Lord
and he will give you
what your heart desires.
FROM PSALM 37:3-4

2 The Lord guides a man
in the way he should go
and protects those who please him.
If they fall they will not stay down,
because the Lord will help them up.
FROM PSALM 37:23-24

3 The Lord saves righteous men
and protects them when trouble comes.
He helps them and rescues them;
he saves them from the wicked,
because they go to him for protection.
FROM PSALM 37:39-40

 Give yourself to the Lord. Trust him and he will
help. He will make your goodness shine like the
midday sun.   FROM PSALM 37:5-6

Flourishing like a tree

Happy is the person who trusts in God. He is like a tree growing near a stream and sending out roots to the water. It is not afraid when hot weather comes, because its leaves stay green. It has no worries if rain does not fall, and it keeps on bearing fruit.   FROM JEREMIAH 17:7-8

1 I am like an olive tree,
   growing in the house of God.
I trust in his constant love always.
FROM PSALM 52:8

2 How happy are those who love to study
   God's word
who meditate on God's law by day and night.
They are like trees that grow beside a stream,
that bear fruit at the right time.
Their leaves do not dry up.
They succeed in everything they do.
FROM PSALM 1:2-3

3 Those who do right will flourish
   like palm trees,
   like Lebanon cedars.
Planted in the Lord's house,
   they will flourish in his grounds,
      staying fresh and green
   and bearing fruit even in old age,
      revealing God's goodness.
FROM PSALM 92:12-15

The ways of Wisdom are pleasant, and lead to contentment: hold onto Wisdom. She will be a tree of life and happiness.   FROM PROVERBS 3:17-18

Strength in God

Lord God, please listen to my prayers. Isolated and depressed, I call on you—lead me to the high rock of safety. For you are my refuge, a strong battlement against the enemy. I want to live close to you all the time, and shelter in the protection of your wings.   FROM PSALM 61:1-4

1 God is our shelter and strength,
always ready to help when trouble comes.
So we will not be afraid
even if earthquakes erupt
and mountains collapse into the ocean,
even if the seas rage
and the hills tremble with their violent power.
FROM PSALM 46:1-3

2 Lord, I do love you.
You alone are my defender.
It is God who protects me.
He is a fortress to me.
With him I feel secure.
God protects me like a shield;
  he is strong;
  he keeps me safe.
FROM PSALM 18:1-2

3 The Lord protects and defends me,
because I trust in him.
FROM PSALM 28:7

 Praise and glory, wisdom and thanksgiving, honour and power and strength belong to God for ever.
FROM REVELATION 7:11

God is trustworthy

Everything God does, all his actions, are perfect. And as for his words, they are totally dependable. He shields everyone who comes to him for protection. Apart from the Lord, there is no one who is God. Our defence and rock is the Lord God. FROM PSALM 18:30-31

1 I trust in God for safety.
How foolish it would be for you to say to me:
'Flee away!
Escape to the mountains!
When all is dark
the wicked are preparing to make war against the good.
What can a good man do
when his world is falling apart?'
Always remember that God watches over everything.
He hates evil and punishes it.
But the good live with him always.
FROM PSALM 11:1-4,7

2 God's promises can be trusted.
They are like silver,
hallmarked and pure,
refined in the hottest furnace.
FROM PSALM 12:6

 In times of difficulty, the Lord is a refuge. Those who know you, Lord, will trust you, for you do not abandon anyone who cares for you.
FROM PSALM 9:9-10

The right way
if we trust

Trust God with your whole heart. Don't rely on your opinions. Remember him in everything you do, and he will guide you on your way. Do not think of yourself as being wiser than you really are. Give evil no elbow room, but fear the Lord.   FROM
PROVERBS 3:5-7

1 Study the teachings of the wise men;
    remember them;
quote them when you can.
I am telling you this
because I want you to put your trust in God.
FROM PROVERBS 22:17-19

2 Those who go to you for strength are
    happy.
Lord God, you make happy
all those who trust in you.
FROM PSALM 84:5,12

3 Protect me, my God.
    I trust you for safety.
To you I say,
    'All good things
    have come from you alone.'
FROM PSALM 16:1-2

This saying is utterly reliable: 'If we have died with Jesus Christ, we will live with him. If we endure to the end, we will reign with him.'
FROM   2 TIMOTHY 2:11-12

I trust in the Lord,
so I will not be afraid

FROM PSALM 56:4

A home with Jesus

Jesus said, 'Do not keep worrying. Trust in God always and trust in me. I am going to prepare a place for you in my Father's many-roomed house. After that I shall return to take you there with me. Where I am, you will always be.   FROM JOHN 14:1-3

1 If anyone loves me,
   he will obey my commands.
Then he will also know my Father's love
and we shall come to him
and make our home with him.
FROM JOHN 14:23

2 Do not let your hearts be troubled or
   afraid.
You heard me say,
'I am going away,
and I am coming back to you.'
FROM JOHN 14:27-28

3 I am coming to you, holy Father.
   Keep those who belong to me safe,
so that they may be one like us.'
FROM JOHN 17:11

 In my vision of the heavenly city, I did not see a temple, because the Lord God and the Lamb are heaven's temple.   FROM REVELATION 21:22

In God's word

I get up before dawn and seek help from God.
It is in your word that I place my complete hope. I lie
awake all night long and think about your promises.
Lord God, you are close at hand and your commands
are true.   FROM PSALM 119:147-148,151

1 Show me how much you love me, my
Lord.
Save me as you promised.
Then I can answer the insults I receive,
because I trust in your word.
FROM PSALM 119:41-42

2 I respect and love your commands.
I reach out for them.
I meditate on your instructions.
FROM PSALM 119:48

3 I wait eagerly for God's help
and I trust in his word.
FROM PSALM 130:5

4 The words of the Lord are true.
Everything God says and does
can be utterly relied upon.
FROM PSALM 33:4

People are like grass and their glory fades like wild
flowers. Grass dies down, and flowers drop their
petals and die off, but the Lord's word goes on for
time and eternity.   FROM 1 PETER 1:24-25

To be strong

Those who trust God are like Mount Zion, God's mountain. It is immoveable; it can never be shaken. As Jerusalem is protected by a circle of mountains, so God's people are protected by the Lord, now and always.   FROM PSALM 125:1-2

1 We put our hope in the Lord.
He is our protector and our helper.
So we are glad because of him.
We trust in his holy name.
FROM PSALM 33:20-21

2 When I am afraid
I put my trust in God.
Then I am no longer afraid.
What can man do to me?
I praise my God
for the promises in his word.
FROM PSALM 56:3-4

3 God is my Saviour.
I trust him and am not afraid.
He gives me power and strength.
FROM ISAIAH 12:2

 The Lord is my rock, my protector and deliverer. He surrounds me like a shield; he defends me from attack. With the Lord I am safe.   FROM PSALM 18:2

E18

Songs of trust

Mary, the mother of Jesus, said: 'My spirit has come alive and my soul praises God. My spirit is overjoyed with my Saviour God. Even though I am only his humble servant, he's remembered me. Everyone who honours him will know his mercy.'   FROM LUKE 1:46-47,50

1 The Lord protects and defends me,
so I trust him.
He gives me help and makes me glad.
I joyfully sing his praise!
FROM PSALM 28:7

2 Some trust in their warheads,
others in their horses,
but we trust in the power of our God.
FROM PSALM 20:7

3 Delight yourself in the Lord
and he will give you
the desires of your heart.
Commit yourself to him,
trust him,
and he will give you your heart-felt wishes.
FROM PSALM 37:3-4

 God's law is perfect, it gives us strength. His word is trustworthy and gives wisdom to those who lack it. God's laws are always right and we are happy when we keep them.   FROM PSALM 19:7,8

Trust in God
who cares for you

Do not act as though you are better than other people. For, as it says in the book of Proverbs, 'God sets his face against the proud, but God freely gives his favour to the humble.' Hand over all your worries to God; he cares for you.   FROM 1 PETER 5:5,7

1 'I don't have any bread,
only a handful of flour and a little oil,'
the widow woman said.
Elijah replied,
'Don't be afraid, for God says,
"The jar of flour will not be used up,
the jug of oil will not run dry,
until the Lord gives rain on the land."'
FROM 1 KINGS 17:12-14

2 Andrew spoke up,
'Here is a boy with five small barley loaves and two small fish. But how far can they go? There are so many people here.'
Jesus took the loaves,
gave thanks and gave them out.
He did the same with the fish,
and the people ate as much as they wanted.
FROM JOHN 6:8-12

 So do not worry saying, 'What shall we eat, drink, wear?' Your heavenly Father knows what you need. If you seek him first of all, he will give you the other things you need.   FROM MATTHEW 6:31-34

E22

Prayers for confidence

Lord, thank you that in your word you tell us to trust in you and you will help us. Increase my faith in you, and enable me to give myself to you. I believe you will watch over me, and that you will always stay with me.
Amen.

Lord, when we trust in you, we grow and flourish in your presence. When we trust in you, you remove all fear from us and protect us like a father protects his children. When we trust in you, you will lead us to safety from our enemies. Thank you, Jesus.
Amen.

My own prayer

_____

_____

_____

Seeds of Security

Calm in a storm

Security in our standing before God

Grasp the fact that through our Lord Jesus Christ, we are made right and stand at peace before God. Through faith we know about God's grace, which we now enjoy. We can even be happy about our difficulties as they produce endurance which improves our characters and this gives us hope.   FROM ROMANS 5:1-4

1 It is not easy to die
even for a good man,
though some have done this.
But what proves God's love to us
is that while we were still sinners,
Jesus Christ died for us.
Now, having died, is it likely
he would fail to save us
from God's righteous anger?
FROM ROMANS 5:7-9

2 Moreover, we should be overjoyed in
God,
through our Lord Jesus Christ,
because he has returned us to himself,
in peace.
FROM ROMANS 5:11

If when we were God's enemies we were made right with him through Jesus' death, think how much more sure is our salvation by the life of Jesus!   FROM ROMANS 5:10

Security of God's Spirit

To prove that you are his sons, God has sent the Spirit of his Son into our hearts: the Spirit cries, 'Abba, Father', and it is this that makes you a son. You are not a slave of sin any more. And if you are a son, then you most certainly are an heir.

FROM GALATIANS 4:6-7

1 We know that God lives in us
and we in him,
because he has given us his Spirit.
FROM 1 JOHN 3:24

2 Let me put it this way:
if you live by the power of the Spirit,
you will not satisfy the desires
of your selfish natures.
The two are opposites:
the Spirit and your lower nature.
Since the Spirit is our life,
be sure to be directed by the Spirit.
FROM GALATIANS 5:16-18

3 May grace be yours,
may peace be yours,
from our Father God
and from the Lord Jesus Christ.
FROM ROMANS 1:7

 Make perfection your aim; have the same goals; be at peace among yourselves. Then God's love and God's peace will be with you. FROM 2 CORINTHIANS 13:11

Security in the Father

John wrote: 'God has poured out his love on us. His love for us is so great that he's made us his children. That's who we really are! Since people don't recognise God, we're not surprised they don't recognise us. When Jesus appears we will be like him.   FROM 1 JOHN 3:1-2

1 Paul wrote:
'Before the world was made
God chose us as his sons
through Christ Jesus.
He has let us know
the mystery of his purposes,
his secret plans made from the beginning.
All human history will culminate in Christ;
everything that exists
in earth and in heaven
is fulfilled in him.
FROM EPHESIANS 1:4,9,10

2 It is in Jesus that we were from the beginning chosen and planned to fit into his will.
You have been stamped
with the seal of the promised Holy Spirit
as a guarantee of your inheritance.
We will take full possession of this pledge
in the day when God's plans are complete,
to the praise of his glory!
FROM EPHESIANS 1:11,13,14

 I will tell others of the Lord's love which never fails. You, Lord God, are our Father. You are the one who has saved us.   FROM ISAIAH 63:7,16

Security in Jesus' return

Jesus said, 'In a short time, you will see me no longer, but then a short time later, you will see me again. For the time being you'll be sad, but I will see you again and your heart will be full of joy which nobody can rob you of.   FROM JOHN 16:16,21

1 Jesus was taken up before their very eyes.
A cloud hid him from sight.
They were staring intently as he was going,
when suddenly two men appeared
dressed in white.
They said, 'Men of Galilee,
why do you stand looking into the sky?
This same Jesus, who was taken into heaven,
will return in the same way.'
FROM ACTS 1:9-11

2 'See. I am coming soon.
I shall be with you again
and will repay everyone
according to his deeds.
I am the first and the last,
the beginning and the end.'
FROM REVELATION 22:12,13

3 Our homeland is in heaven.
We await our Lord Jesus Christ,
our Saviour,
who comes from there.
FROM PHILIPPIANS 3:20

 There will be a loud command, the archangel's voice and God's trumpet. Then the Lord himself will come down from heaven and we will be with him for ever.   FROM 1 THESSALONIANS 4:16-17

Security in God's love

Jesus said: 'Everyone whom the Father gives to me will come to me. I will never drive anyone away who comes to me. I've come from heaven to do God's will, and it is his will that I should never let go of anyone he has given me. I will raise them up to life on the last day.'   FROM JOHN 6:37-39

1 I am absolutely sure of this:
   nothing can separate us
from the Love of God seen in Jesus Christ,
   neither death
      nor life,
   neither angels, nor powers in heaven,
   neither present, nor future things,
   neither height, nor depth nor anything
whatever in creation.
FROM ROMANS 8:38-39

2 No one has ever seen God.
   That is quite true.
But if we love each other,
then God will live in our hearts
and his love in us
will grow to perfection.
FROM 1 JOHN 4:12-13

Nothing can separate us from the love of God. Nothing—not life nor death, angels, nor powers—nothing at all can cut us off from God's love in our Lord Jesus Christ.
FROM ROMANS 8:38-39

God has said,
'I will never abandon you.'
FROM HEBREWS 13:5

Security in the Creator God

Look at the stars and remember who created them. You should never say that the Lord doesn't care about you or bother if you're in trouble. Have you forgotten that the Lord is the everlasting God? He's made the whole world.   FROM ISAIAH 40:26-28

1 God created man from the earth's dust
breathing life into his form,
and man became a living being,
made in God's image.
FROM GENESIS 2:7

2 The Creator God,
who made everything in the world,
is Lord of heaven and earth.
He is completely self-sufficient,
lacking nothing,
for life itself belongs to him,
and is given to him.
Our Creator God is not far from us:
it is within him alone that we live and move.
Our very selves exist because of him.
FROM ACTS 17:24-25,27-28

Let us go and worship our Maker. Let us kneel and sing praises to him, for he is our God and we are his people.   FROM PSALM 95:6,7

Security in
the eternal Creator

The Lord says: 'I am the Alpha and the Omega, the first and the last. I am the Mighty One who is, who was and who is to come. Don't be afraid. I am the Living One who has come alive. Yes, I was dead once, but now I am alive and will be alive for ever.   FROM REVELATION 1:8, 17-18

1 In the beginning
God laid the earth's foundations
and made heaven.
These things will come to an end,
but the creator God will remain.
His creations will wear out
like garments which we change and discard.
But the Creator is eternal,
the same unchanging God for ever.
FROM PSALM 102:25, 27

2 John wrote:
'Then I heard every creature
in heaven,
on earth,
in the world,
in the whole universe,
singing.
"To him who sits on the throne,
and to the Lamb of God,
be praise, honour, glory, and might."'
FROM REVELATION 5:13

 God has said, 'I will never desert you. I will never abandon you.' So with complete confidence we can say, 'My help comes from the Lord.'   FROM HEBREWS 13:5-6

Security in God's way

God's solid foundation stone stands with this double inscription: 'The Lord knows who beongs to him', and, 'Everyone who claims to belong to God has no dealings with wrongdoing.'   FROM
2 TIMOTHY 2:19

1 Let us have done with all the wrong things
that clutter our lives.
Let us throw off the bad habits
that keep tripping us up,
and let us run steadily to Jesus,
looking straight at him.
He is the one who started us off.
And he will make sure that
we are able to finish.
FROM HEBREWS 12:1-2

2 From the day we first met,
you have helped me spread
the good news about Jesus.
I really am grateful to God for you.
I know that God will stay with you
right to the end.
He will finish the good work
he started in you.
FROM PHILIPPIANS 1:4-6

 God is compassionate. You can stop your crying now because he longs to be kind to you. As soon as you seek his help he'll answer you.
FROM ISAIAH   30:18-19

Security in the light of God's Son

God is light. No darkness at all exists in him. So we lie when we live in darkness but say we are living in God's presence. However, if we do live in the light, as God does, then we have fellowship with each other and forgiveness of our sins because of the death of his Son Jesus.   FROM 1 JOHN 1:5-7

1 The same Creator God, who said,
'Let light shine out of darkness',
has shone in our hearts
giving us the light of the knowledge
of God's glory
seen in the face of Jesus Christ.
FROM 2 CORINTHIANS 4:6

2 The true light that brings light to
mankind was coming into the world.
The Word of God came alive in the flesh
and lived among us on earth,
full of grace and truth.
We have seen his glory.
This glory is of the only Son
of the heavenly Father.
FROM JOHN 1:9,14

 Jesus said: 'I am the light of the world. Everyone who follows me will live in the light. He won't be walking in the darkness. His life will be in the light.'   FROM JOHN 8:12

Security in God's power

Jesus is alive for ever and he is able to save completely those who come to God through him because he is praying for them, and because he offered up himself as the one and only sacrifice for everyone.   FROM HEBREWS 7:24-25, 27

1 God will change these human bodies
into a form resembling his own
glorious body,
by the same power by which he brings
the whole universe under his control.
FROM PHILIPPIANS 3:21

2 We are God's work of art,
created anew in Jesus Christ,
to live out those good works
which he intended us to do
from the beginning.
FROM EPHESIANS 2:10

3 We who have this treasure
are like ordinary jars of clay,
showing clearly that
this overwhelming power belongs to God
and not to us.
FROM 2 CORINTHIANS 4:7

Glory be to God who is able to keep you from falling
and to bring you safely into his glorious presence,
faultless and full of joy.   FROM JUDE 24

Prayers for security

I thank you, Lord, for all the promises you have
made, none of which is ever broken. I praise you for
the utter reliability of those promises you made to all
your children, and for the knowledge that you will
fulfil them all.
Amen.

We thank you, Jesus, that you are the sure foundation
on which we can build our lives. And we thank you
that you will never stop caring for us. We know we
can securely place our treasure in heaven, knowing
that it will never be taken from us.
Amen.

My own prayer

_____

_____

_____

Seeds of Comfort

Under his shadow

The promise of comfort

The Lord Almighty says, 'These cities will be prosperous once more. The Lord will select Jerusalem as his own city, and Jerusalem will know the Lord's comfort.'   FROM ZECHARIAH 1:17

1 You have heard of the patience of Job.
He stood firm
and God blessed him in the end;
God is full of loving sympathy and mercy.
FROM JAMES 5:11

2 'Comfort my people; comfort them,'
says God.
'Speak to them with tenderness.
Tell them that their strife is over.
Their sin has been pardoned by God.
FROM ISAIAH 40:1-2

3 The Lord will comfort his people.
He will make a garden
out of the dry barren land.
Joy and gladness will be there;
singing and praise will be heard.
FROM ISAIAH 51:3

 Our hope for you is well founded because we know that as you share our sufferings you will, in the same way, share in our comfort, which is from God.   FROM 2 CORINTHIANS 1:7

God's comfort is unfailing

Because of God's great love we are not
destroyed. His loving understanding never fails. It is
new every morning. Because the Lord is all I want in
life, I put my trust in him.   FROM LAMENTATIONS
3:22-24

1 God says,
'I am the one who brings you comfort.'
FROM ISAIAH 51:12

2 Shout for joy, heaven above!
Rejoice, earth!
Burst into song, mountains!
Because it is God himself
who comforts his people.
It is he who has compassion on the suffering.
FROM ISAIAH 49:13

3 The Lord says:
'I have seen how they have turned against
me but I will heal them.
I will guide them,
and look after them and console them.'
FROM ISAIAH 57:18

 I must praise the Lord and never forget how
wonderful he is. As a father has compassion on his
children, so the Lord comforts those who are
his.   FROM PSALM 103:2,13

Comfort of the needy

He has sent me to bind up the broken-hearted, to proclaim freedom and release to prisoners. He has sent me to preach the good news to the poor, since I have been filled with the Spirit of the Lord Almighty.   FROM ISAIAH 61:1-3

1 The Lord upholds the cause of the victimised.
He feeds the hungry.
He sets prisoners free,
gives the blind their sight.
It is the Lord who lifts up
those who are bowed down
and he watches over the strangers.
He provides for the fatherless and the widows.
He defeats the plans of evil men.
The Lord God reigns supreme for ever.
His rule never ends.
FROM PSALM 146:7-10

2 Girls will dance and be glad.
Old men and young men alike will rejoice.
I, the Lord, will turn their mourning
into happiness.
In place of sorrow
I will give them comfort and joy.
FROM JEREMIAH 31:13

You ruins of Jerusalem burst into songs of joy, for the Lord rescues Jerusalem, and comforts his people.   FROM ISAIAH 52:9

Like a shepherd

The Lord is my shepherd and he will give me everything I need. He brings me to green fields and leads me to refreshing pools of water. He shows me the correct path to take.   FROM PSALM 23:1-4

1 I am the good shepherd.
I know my own and my own know me,
just as the Father knows me,
and I know my Father.
I lay down my life for my sheep.
FROM JOHN 10:14,15

2 'He who scattered his people
will gather them together again.
He will watch over his flock
like a shepherd,' says God.
FROM JEREMIAH 31:10

3 'I will look after my sheep,' says the
Lord. 'I will hunt for thew lost and bring
back the strays.
I will bind up the injured
and strengthen the weak.
The sick ones I will heal.'
FROM EZEKIEL 34:15-16

The Lamb who sits on the throne will be their shepherd and will lead them to springs of fresh water; and God will wipe all tears from their eyes.   FROM REVELATION 7:11

Like a parent

The Lord says, 'You will be like a child, that is nursed by its mother, carried in her arms and treated with love. I will comfort you, as a mother comforts her child.' FROM ISAIAH 66:13

1 'Can a mother forget the baby at her breast
and have no love for the baby she gave birth to?
Though even she may forget her baby
I will not forget you,' says the Lord.
I can never forget you,
your names are engraved on the palms of my hands—
that's how much you mean to me.
FROM ISAIAH 49:15,16

2 Which of you fathers would give your son a snake if he asked for a fish to eat?
Or would give a scorpion when he asks for an egg?
Even you, who are evil,
give good things to your children.
Don't you see how much more
your heavenly Father
will give the Holy Spirit to you if you ask him?
FROM LUKE 11:11-13

The Father has lavished his love on us. His love is so great that he has made us his children.   FROM 1 JOHN 3:1

Give thanks to God in every situation
FROM 1 THESSALONIANS 5:18

Protection
brings comfort

Lord God, I know that you will always listen to the prayers of my heart. Show me now the wonder of your great love. You save all who take refuge in you. Cherish me, as people cherish their eyesight. Hide me in the shadow of your wing.   FROM
PSALM 17:7-8

1 You can say of the Lord,
'He is my refuge and fortress,
my God whom I trust.'
He will save you from deadly snares.
Just as a bird cares for its young
he hides you with his feathers
and keeps you safe under his wings.
FROM PSALM 91:2-4

2 God said to his people:
'You have seen how I carried you
as on eagles' wings,
and brought you to myself.'
FROM EXODUS 19:4

3 Jesus looked at the city sadly:
'Jerusalem, Jerusalem,
I longed to gather your children together,
as a hen gathers her chicks under her wings,
but you would not let me.'
FROM LUKE 13:34

 How priceless your constant love is, Lord God!
People from all walks of life find safety in the shadow
of your wings.   FROM PSALM 36:7

Longing for God's comfort

May your unfailing love be my comfort as you promised. May your compassion come to me that I may live, my God. I take great delight in your commands; save me, for I belong to you.
FROM PSALM 119:76-77,94

1 Give me a sign of your goodness
to warn off my enemies.
You, Lord, have helped me and comforted me.
FROM PSALM 86:17

2 Your compassion is abundant, my Lord.
Give me new life, as you promised.
FROM PSALM 119:156

3 From the day I was born
I have relied on you, Lord.
I have always put my trust in you.
Now that I am in serious trouble,
with nobody to help me,
please keep close to me.
You are my strength
and you quickly come to my aid.
You are not far from me.
FROM PSALM 22:10-11,19

 Although you were angry with me, Lord, your anger has turned from me, and you have comforted me. Lord God, I needn't be frightened because I trust in you, my Saviour.   FROM ISAIAH 12:1-2

Comforting others

When all others had deserted the mugged man, the passing Samaritan felt sorry for him. He broke his journey and went over to him, he put oil and wine on his wounds and then he bandaged him and took care of him.   FROM LUKE 10:33-35

1 Praise God, the Father of our Lord Jesus. He is the Father of compassion
and the God of all comfort.
He comforts us in our troubles,
so that we in turn can comfort others in difficulty with the same comfort that comes from him.
FROM 2 CORINTHIANS 1:3-4

2 So, God's chosen people, holy and dearly loved as you are,
put on the clothes of compassion,
kindness,
humility,
gentleness,
patience.
FROM COLOSSIANS 3:12

3 Rejoice with people who are rejoicing; mourn with people who are mourning.
FROM ROMANS 12:15

If you receive strength from belonging to Christ, if his love comforts you, if you enjoy the companionship of his Spirit, then offer to other Christians that same comfort and love.
FROM PHILIPPIANS 2:1-2

Comfort
through others

The more that we ourselves share in Christ's sufferings, the more we are able to pass on to others Christ's comforting power. So when we go through suffering it is so you can experience comfort and have strength to face similar trials.   FROM
2 CORINTHIANS 1:5-6

1 God, who comforts the downcast,
comforted us by Titus' coming
and by the greetings of love
he passed on to us from all of you.
FROM 2 CORINTHIANS 7:6-7

2 Paul wrote to his friend Timothy,
'Do your best to come to me quickly. I am alone except for Luke who has stayed with me. Try and bring Mark along with you when you come, as he's a great help to me.'
FROM 2 TIMOTHY 4:9-11

3 Paul wrote,
'Aristarchus, Mark and Justus send you their greetings.
They are here in prison with me
and have proved such a comfort to me.'
FROM COLOSSIANS 4:10,11

 At last Paul arrived in Rome. The Roman Christians came out as far as the Three Inns to meet him. This lifted Paul's spirits, and he thanked God.
FROM ACTS 28:11-15

Jesus comforts others

When Jesus saw the leper kneeling in front of him, saying, 'You can heal me if you want to,' Jesus' heart went out to him and he was filled with compassion. So Jesus said, 'Of course I want to. You are cured!' And at once the man was free from leprosy.   FROM MARK 1:41-42

1 Jesus looked at Mary and Martha
     when they told him Lazarus was dead.
He was deeply moved by their sadness.
With a deep heart-felt sigh
he asked to be shown to Lazarus' tomb.
Jesus wept.
FROM JOHN 11:33-35

2 Unless I go the Counsellor,
     the one who comforts and strengthens you,
will not come to you;
but if I go, I will send him to you.
He will lead you into all truth.
FROM JOHN 16:7,13

Two blind men called out to Jesus, 'Take pity on us.' Jesus stopped and called them to him. When he saw them he was filled with compassion. He touched their eyes and healed them.
FROM MATTHEW 20:30-34

Prayers for comfort

I praise you, heavenly Father, that even in my greatest
trials you are always with me. Thank you for the
strength you give me when times are hard. I pray that
I will never forget the comfort you can give me.
Thank you that all I have to do is to ask.
Amen.

Lord, thank you for promising in your word to look
after us, as a shepherd looks after his sheep. We pray
that we may show the same care and love to others in
trouble. Teach us how to be compassionate at all
times, even to our enemies. Help us to take our
example from you.
Amen.

My own prayer

_____

_____

_____

$\mathcal{S}$eeds of Thanks

Counting our blessings

Thanks for what God has done

God's rule is stong and totally reliable.
Therefore let us express our deep gratitude to God
and make our worship pleasing to him. We worship
him with deep reverence in our hearts.   FROM
HEBREWS 12:28

1 I have so much to thank you for, Lord
God.
My heart overflows with praise
for all you have done.
Your wisdom is too deep to fathom
and your actions defy description.
FROM PSALM 92:1,4-5

2 The Lord wants you to give him due
honour
and to carry out his wishes.
He wants you to love him
and to do all you can for him;
to keep his laws and his directions for living.
God is the one to praise;
he has done all these wonderful things for you.
FROM DEUTERONOMY 10:12-13,21

God's love and compassion go out to the whole
creation; all the creatures he has made praise him; all
the people created by him give thanks to
him. FROM PSALM 145:9,10

Thanks for finished work

God created mankind in his own image. He made them male and female. God looked at everything he had made, and he was very pleased with it. The sixth morning and evening came and the creation of the whole world was finished.

FROM GENESIS 1:27,31-2:1

1 All the people praised God
when he rescued them from slavery.
Their leader, Moses, sang,
'I'll sing to the Lord who has saved me.
He is my strength and my song
and now he's become my deliverer.
His constant love guides those he has rescued.'

FROM EXODUS 15:1-2,13

2 At the dedication of the Temple,
Solomon prayed:
'Nobody on earth or in heaven is like you,
Lord God.
With your followers who go all the way with
you, you show unfailing love.
The promise you gave to my father David has
come true.'

FROM 1 KINGS 8:22-24

 Jesus Christ made a spectacular offering of himself. As God had planned, he died for each one of us. So we have been cleared from sin.   FROM HEBREWS 10:10

Thanks for God's love

Let everyone who trusts God sing his praises.
Sing a new song of praise to the Lord. Remember, the
Lord lavishes his love on his people. Left to ourselves
we amount to very little, but we have salvation from
God.   FROM PSALM 149:1,4

1 I am grateful to the Lord Jesus
because he gives me strength.
How wonderful that he has seen fit
to select me so that I can serve him.
FROM 1 TIMOTHY 1:12

2 The Holy Spirit filled Jesus with joy and
he said,
'Lord of the created world,
I give you thanks, my Father,
that your truth is masked from the clever
but is clear to those who trust you
with the complete dependence of a child.
FROM LUKE 10:21

3 Because God is so wonderful,
give him thanks.
His love is for ever.
We praise him as the great God,
the mighty Lord.
His love is constant.
FROM PSALM 136:1-2,25-26

How wonderful God is. Let everyone give thanks to
him. His love goes on and on; it never comes to an
end.   FROM 1 CHRONICLES 16:34

Thanks for healing

Out of the ten men Jesus had healed, only one came back. He threw himself at Jesus' feet and praised God. Jesus said, 'Weren't there ten cured? What about the others? Has only this foreigner from Samaria returned to give thanks?'   FROM LUKE 17:15-18

1 When Jesus came to the tomb of Lazarus,
he looked to heaven and prayed,
'I thank you, Father,
for hearing my prayer.'
Then Jesus spoke out loudly,
'Lazarus, get up. Leave your tomb
and come here.'
And the dead Lazarus got up,
still wrapped in his grave clothes.
Jesus said, 'Unwrap these grave clothes
and let him go free.'
FROM JOHN 11:41-44

2 As soon as the blind man was healed by
Jesus, he praised God and joined up with
Jesus' followers.
Everyone who witnessed this healing
also gave thanks to God for him.
FROM LUKE 18:43

 Praise the Lord. It's a good thing to sing God's praises. He heals broken hearts, he bandages up the injured. It's only right to give thanks to God.   FROM PSALM 147:1-3

Thanks for each other

I'll tell you why I never cease giving thanks to God for you. It's because of your trust in the Lord Jesus and because of your love for all Christians. That's why I always remember you in my prayers.   FROM EPHESIANS 1:15-16

1 As we pray for each of you,
   we do so with hearts full of thanks to God.
Before our God and Father we remember your faith, love and hope.
Your faith is put into practice;
your love is behind all your work,
and your hope is pinned
on the Lord Jesus Christ.
FROM 1 THESSALONIANS 1:2-3

2 God's loving kindness has come to you
   through Jesus Christ.
That's why I'm always giving thanks to God for you.
As a result of your life with Jesus Christ
you have become spiritually wealthy,
especially in your mind and in your speaking.
FROM 1 CORINTHIANS 1:4-5

 I give thanks to Jesus Christ for you all. I thank him that from far and wide people speak well of your faith.   FROM ROMANS 1:8

*G*od's compassion never fails
FROM LAMENTATIONS 3:23

Thanks for Jesus' death for us

Isaac asked his father, 'I can see the wood and the fire, but where's the lamb for the burnt offering? Abraham said, 'Don't worry. God will provide the lamb.' ...Then Abraham saw a ram caught up by its horns in a bush. FROM GENESIS 22:7-8

1 He was wounded because of all the things we have done wrong.
He was beaten for our crimes.
He was punished.
Because he went through all this—
we can be healed.
FROM ISAIAH 53:5

2 During the meal Jesus picked up the cup, said a prayer of thanks to God over it, and passed it round to his disciples saying, 'Drink from this cup, all of you.
This is my blood
which sets the seal
on God's special agreement.
My blood is poured out so that many people can have forgiveness.
FROM MATTHEW 26:27-28

 Jesus Christ offered for all time one sacrifice for sins. Then after he had finished he sat down at God's right hand. FROM HEBREWS 10:12

Thanks for friends

Pass on my very best wishes to Priscilla and Aquila who have worked alongside me in our service for Jesus Christ. I'm completely in their debt since they even risked their lives for me. FROM ROMANS 16:3-4

1 Daniel shared his problem
with his three friends,
Hananiah, Mishael and Azariah.
He begged them to pray
that God would have mercy on them,
and that they should be granted
a stay of execution
FROM DANIEL 2:17-18

2 When the Christians in Rome heard that
we were about to arrive in Rome, they
came out as far as the market of Appius and
the Three Inns.
The sight of them lifted Paul's spirits and he
thanked God.
FROM ACTS 18:18

3 We were down in the dumps,
but God sent Titus,
who cheered us up.
It wasn't just that we were pleased to see him,
but that he told us how much you love us.
FROM 2 CORINTHIANS 7:6-7

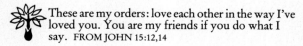 These are my orders: love each other in the way I've loved you. You are my friends if you do what I say. FROM JOHN 15:12,14

Thanks from the heart

Lord, you have transformed my crying into a joyful dance. My sorrow has been replaced by happiness. I'll give voice to my joy with happy songs to God. I will keep on giving thanks to you, for you are my God.   FROM PSALM 30:11-12

1 When I called on you for help, Lord
God, you healed me.
You saved me from going under;
you spared my life.
All of God's people sing the Lord's praises.
FROM PSALM 30:2-4

2 Christ gives us peace and this peace
should direct your decision making.
God has planned that you should live
in harmony together.
You must always have grateful hearts.
May Christ's words be in your deepest
thoughts all the time.
In fact you shouldn't do anything unless it is
in the name of the Lord Jesus.
It is through him that you give thanks
to God the Father.
FROM COLOSSIANS 3:15-17

 God has answered my prayers. God is my Saviour. So I will always be saying thank you to God.   FROM PSALM 118:21,28

H18

Thanks for Jesus Christ

Death gets its power from sin. Sin gets its strength from the law. But death will disappear and we will no longer be judged by the law. So hurrah for Jesus! For he's the one who makes us win through, and we thank God for him. FROM 1 CORINTHIANS 15:56-57

1 Thanks be to God who enables us to be part of his victory procession because we are united to Christ.
God uses us to spread the message about Christ. It's like a sweet scent permeating the whole world.
FROM 2 CORINTHIANS 2:14-15

2 Inside me there is a battle raging.
On the one hand I long to keep God's law,
but on the other hand,
I find that sin is still making me its slave. I feel terrible about this.
I need someone to come along and rescue me from this slavery.
So thanks be to God who has liberated me through our Lord Jesus Christ.
FROM ROMANS 7:24-25

Simeon took the baby Jesus in his arms and thanked God. He said, 'Now I have seen the Deliverer. I have seen how you plan to save the world.'
FROM LUKE 2:28-31

Thanks all the time

Be overflowing with melody and song. Sing hymns, psalms and choruses when you meet with other Christians, and sing in your heart to God. Always give thanks to God the Father in everything, no matter what happens, in the name of our Lord Jesus Christ. FROM EPHESIANS 5:19-20

1 In the middle of the people
I will praise you, Lord God.
I will give thanks to you in front of them all.
FROM PSALM 35:18

2 King David praised God
in front of all the people, saying,
'Lord God you are the God of my ancestor
Jacob, may your name always be praised.
You are powerful and wonderful.
You rule over the whole world.
In fact, everything in heaven and on earth
belongs to you.
FROM 1 CHRONICLES 29:10-13

3 In heaven they worship God saying,
'You are the Lord Almighty.
You exist now, and you always will exist.
Thank you for your rule
of absolute power throughout the world.
FROM REVELATION 11:17

 Pray all the time. Give thanks to God in every situation. God wants you to live like this, depending completely on Jesus. FROM 1 THESSALONIANS 5:18

Prayers of thanks

Lord, I thank you that you gave your only Son to be killed on a cross for me. I cannot understand how it is that he should die for me, sinful and unworthy as I am. But you gave your Son Jesus, out of love for me, and in that knowledge I can do nothing else but praise you.
Amen.

Lord, you have done so much for us, that our own humble offerings look quite insignificant in return. Lord, you deserve our constant thanks and praise. We lift our hearts to you and shout your praises in the hearing of everybody, because you deserve it. Thank you, Lord.
Amen.

My own prayer

_____

_____

_____